Mountain Calling: A Family's Bold Escape from City Life

"A True Story of Struggles and New Beginnings"

Author: Love Kumar [Punjabi Trekker]

YouTube

https://www.youtube.com/@LovesFarm
https://www.youtube.com/@PunjabiTrekker

Insta

https://www.instagram.com/LovesFarmStay

Author Contact: PunjabiTrekker@Gmail.com

ISBN: 978-93-343-9172-5

9 789334 391725

About the Author

Love Kumar, widely recognized as *Punjabi Trekker* on YouTube, is a storyteller, traveller, and advocate for slow, meaningful living. After years of urban life, he and his family made the life-changing decision to leave the chaos of the city and start anew in the mountains.

In their remote village home, Love Kumar balances farming, homestay hosting, and content creation, documenting not just the beauty but also the realities of mountain life. His YouTube channel, *Punjabi Trekker*, has become a source of inspiration for thousands who dream of living closer to nature.

When he isn't tending to his land or filming, Love enjoys quiet walks with his children, working on DIY projects around the house, and watching the sun set behind the hills he now calls home.

Mountain Calling is his heartfelt tribute to courage, family, and the transformative power of nature.

Dedication

This book is lovingly dedicated to my parents,
Mr. Mahesh Chander and **Mrs. Meena Kumari**.

Your faith in me has been the anchor through every storm, your blessings the light that guided me on unknown paths, and your silent sacrifices the strength behind every step of this journey. Without your love and support, the story written in these pages would have remained only a dream.

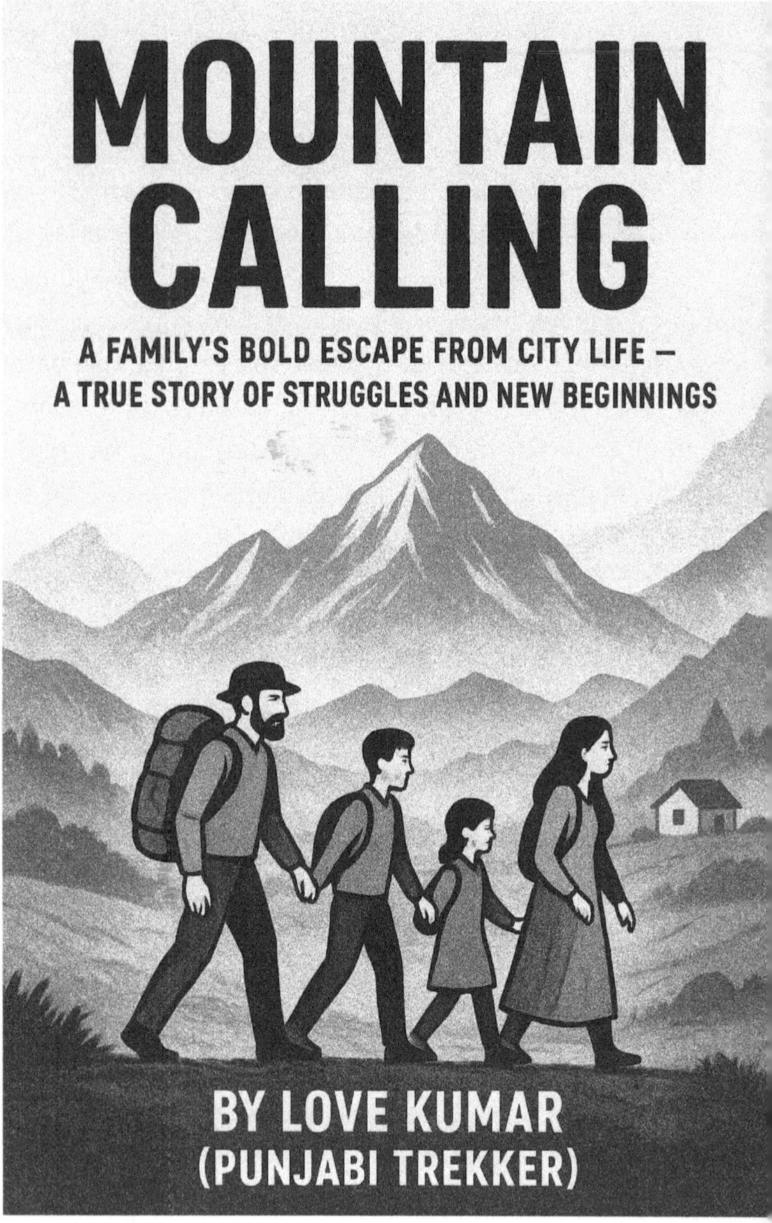
MOUNTAIN CALLING
A FAMILY'S BOLD ESCAPE FROM CITY LIFE –
A TRUE STORY OF STRUGGLES AND NEW BEGINNINGS
BY LOVE KUMAR
(PUNJABI TREKKER)

Introduction: The Dream and The Decision

"You're lucky to live here," people often say when they visit our little farm in the hills.

And maybe I am. But luck had little to do with it. This life — surrounded by nature, far from city noise, full of hard work and slow joy — took courage, mistakes, and learning things the hard way.

Like many others, I once lived in the noise: deadlines, rent, traffic, scrolling. I thought about escaping — but always wondered: *"What will I do there?" "How will I earn?" "Will my children miss out?"*

This book is my honest answer to those questions.

I'm not here to sell a fantasy. Mountain life is not a postcard. It's beautiful, yes — but it's also muddy, cold, uncertain, and deeply humbling.

But if you feel that quiet pull toward the hills... if you dream of growing your food, raising your kids around trees instead of screens, waking up to birdsong instead of alarms — then I wrote this for you.

In these pages, I'll share everything I've learned.

This is our journey. This is our truth. This is the call we answered. This is not a travel book.

It's a transition guide. From fast to slow. From noise to meaning.

– From our family to yours, with love and hope

Contents

Chapter 1: The Calling

Why Some of Us Are Drawn to the Mountains — and What That Means

I still remember one particular evening in our city home. The traffic outside droned on endlessly, my eyes burned from staring at the screen, and the air in the room felt stale. I asked myself quietly:

"Is this really how I want to live the next 20 years?" That was the first time I truly heard it — the whisper.

The Whisper Within

You're not crazy for wanting to leave the city.
You're not the only one who dreams of open skies, crisp mountain air, and mornings where the first sound you hear is birdsong instead of horns.
Every year, thousands of people feel an itch they can't quite name. Some call it "burnout." Some call it "needing a break." Some just say, "I'm tired of this life."

But deep down, it's more than that. It's a calling — a quite longing to return to something more real.

Maybe you've felt it after a trip to the hills, when the silence clings to you long after you're back in traffic. Or maybe it came on a sleepless night in your city home, when you found yourself wondering, *"Is this really all life is? Deadlines, bills, and notifications?"*

For me, it had been there all along, hiding behind every short trip to the hills. Each time we visited, the slowness, the green valleys, and the warmth of village life left a mark. The feeling always lingered long after we returned.

Yet it wasn't until that one evening, staring out of my city home window, that I realised:

The whisper wasn't going away.

💭 What the Calling Sounds Like

The calling is not loud. It never shouts but it whispers.

"I want to grow my own food."
"I want to hear birds, not horns."
"I want my children to know the names of trees, not just brands."
"I want nature's fresh air and pure water to truly feel alive."

For some, this whisper feels like a passing fantasy. For others, it grows louder, becoming a need that refuses to be ignored. And yet — very few acts on it. Why?

The Doubts that Follow

Because as soon as the dream takes shape, the doubts arrive.

"How will I earn a living?"
"What about my children's school?"
"Will there be hospitals nearby?"
"Is this just a romantic idea that will collapse when reality sets in?"

I wrestled with these too. My wife and I had long conversations, sometimes late into the night. Could we really raise children in the hills? Could we survive without the conveniences we'd always known? What if it all went wrong?

These doubts are not bad — they are part of the process. The calling is not meant to lure you blindly; it is meant to make you search for truth.

If you are asking these questions, you are already on the right path. They don't mean your dream is foolish. They mean you are preparing to look at it honestly. This book will not try to convince you that mountain life is perfect. It isn't.

The mountains can be harsh, unpredictable, and demanding. But they are also deeply honest. They strip away pretenses. They remind you of what matters.

Here, life gives you something the city rarely offers — perspective. You begin to notice the sound of silence, the taste of real food, the beauty of slowness, and even your own forgotten thoughts.

🌱 Who Is This Life For?

This life is not for everyone. It calls only to those who:

Don't mind getting their hands dirty.
Can live without instant results.
Are ready to slow down... but not give up.
Seek peace more than convenience.
Want roots more than reach.

If that sounds like you, then you are already halfway to the mountains — even if you are still sitting in a city apartment right now.

⚡ A Gentle Warning

Many YouTube videos and Instagram reels make mountain life look like a permanent vacation — misty mornings, cozy cups of chai, endless views of snow-capped peaks. That is part of the story, but not the whole truth.

The other side looks like this:

Nights when the power is out for three days straight.

When the only water source freezes in mid-winter.

When a cow escapes and tramples your field overnight.

When you earn nothing for months and wonder if you made a mistake.

But then there are moments that no city can give you:

Cooking on a wood-fire while rain taps on your tin roof.

Drinking tea outside while your children run barefoot on the soil.

Learning to fix things with your hands instead of your wallet.

Watching the sky turn orange, with nothing but the sound of wind around you.

That's the mountain calling. It is not glamorous. It is not easy. But it is true. And if you feel it — really feel it — then welcome. You are already part of a story much bigger than yourself.

Chapter 2: Escaping the Corporate Cage

Road to financial freedom

I grew up in a middle-class Indian family where the primary focus was always on survival—earning enough to cover food, housing, bills, and education, with just a little thought spared for the future.

We lived hand to mouth, with no savings. My father ran a small tailoring shop in Delhi and would ride his bicycle 10 kilometres each day to and from work.

Despite our limited means, my parents ensured that we never lacked the essentials—food, shelter, and education were always provided. Luxuries like cars or even a motorbike were far beyond our reach.

As the eldest of three siblings, the weight of expectation fell naturally on my shoulders. After completing my education in software engineering, I landed a job in an MNC. That moment brought a sense of hope and anticipation for a better life to my entire family.

With hard work, persistence, and a bit of luck, I quickly progressed in my career—eventually becoming a technical team manager and earning a handsome salary.

One of the proudest moments of my life was when we bought a villa in a prestigious neighbourhood in Gurgaon with the help of a loan. I remember celebrating with my father—we shared our first beer together, and his eyes shone with happiness. That evening, surrounded by family and friends, we danced in our new home. There was joy in the air.

With time, I bought a car, got married, and later left the MNC to join a startup as a technical architect, seeking new challenges and opportunities to grow. After our wedding, my love for travel blossomed. Our honeymoon in Shimla sparked a passion for the hills, nature, wildlife, and the charm of slow-paced village life. I often found myself wishing, during evening drives home from work, that the road would somehow lead me into the mountains.

But corporate life had its constraints—limited vacations and growing responsibilities. Nighttime calls for technical emergencies disturbed my sleep, and over time, I began to feel creatively stagnant in my management role. Craving change and inspired by a desire for a more meaningful, peaceful life, I made a bold decision: I quit my job, even with only modest savings, a joint family to support, loans to repay, and two young children.

I launched an e-commerce business selling authentic Indian Ayurvedic products to an international market. With my technical background and the support of my brother, the venture grew quickly. Our initial goal was a modest ₹30,000 per month—just enough to cover our expenses—but soon the income exceeded that of my previous job.

Yoga and pranayama became part of my daily routine, helping me find peace amidst the chaos of modern life. My family stood by my decision to take the leap into entrepreneurship. The risk paid off—I gained not just financial freedom but also the freedom of time. With a stable internet connection, I could work from anywhere, which allowed me to finally plan a life closer to nature.

Chapter 3: The First Leap - Journey begins

From the City to the Hills — A Family's Leap of Faith

People often ask me, *"What made you leave everything and come to the mountains?"*

I smile, because there isn't just one reason. It wasn't a sudden decision. It was years of small whispers that slowly became too loud to ignore.

Life Before the Mountains

Leaving behind our city home was harder than I expected. On the surface, it was just four walls. But within those walls were years of routines, memories, comfort zones.

Every corner had a story — the dining table where we laughed, the balcony where we sipped tea while planning a future we weren't sure of, the children's room where toys were scattered like confetti.

And yet, all of it had started to feel suffocating. I would sit in that same balcony and stare at the traffic, thinking, *"Is this the life we will live forever? Will my children grow up only knowing concrete, deadlines, and malls?"*

One night, after the kids had gone to bed, my wife and I sat down at the dining table. We spoke about the idea of moving. Could we really do it? Could we raise our kids away from malls and screens? Could we live without the instant comforts of the city?

The questions were endless.
The fear was real.
The heart knew the answer, even when the mind resisted, but then came the thought that changed everything:

"If it doesn't work, we can always come back. But if we never try, we'll always regret it."

We had to try..

When the Dream Began

Every big journey begins with a small, shaky step. For us, that step was not buying land or building a house. It was simply renting a small place in the mountains — a trial year to test if we could really do this.

We didn't pack up overnight. We began small. We started researching mountain regions, their weather, schools, hospitals, and — most importantly — income possibilities.

I still remember walking through villages with my kids. They ran excitedly through fields, pointed at cows, asked endless questions about goats and streams.

My wife spoke to locals about winters, schools, and daily life. I just stood there, watching, thinking: *This feels like life.*

We began with research — places, weather, accessibility, schools, and possible income sources.
We visited different villages, spoke to locals, asked the uncomfortable questions.

During one of my cycling trips through Uttarakhand, I came across a small village on my way back. Something about the place immediately spoke to me— it had a quiet charm, a simplicity that felt like home. While chatting with a local villager, I was introduced to a homeowner who was renting out a two-bedroom floor at a very reasonable price. The house was just a short distance from the nearest town, yet it felt worlds away—nestled beside a gentle stream and surrounded by fields of blooming lilies.

Eventually, we found a small village in the hills. Peaceful, a little remote, but promising. It wasn't perfect, but it felt right.

I couldn't stop thinking about the place. After discussing it with my wife and parents, we made a decision that felt bold but right—we rented the home. At the time, my elder son had just started attending play school in the city, and my daughter was still too young for school. It felt like the perfect moment to take a break from the city's chaos and immerse ourselves in the rhythms of village life.

So, we moved—our whole family—to this peaceful hill home, eager to experience the authenticity and stillness that only rural life could offer.

We rented a home and committed to one year — not forever. Just a test.

The Mountain Trial

When we first rented a house in the hills, everything felt strange. The walls smelled of pine wood instead of paint. Nights were dark — *really* dark — the kind of blackness the city never knows. The silence was so thick it felt alive.

That first week, we struggled. We lit candles when the electricity went. We boiled extra water for drinking because we weren't sure of the supply. The children asked, "When will we go back?" My wife quietly wondered if we had been reckless.

Even small things became adventures — and sometimes frustrations. The village shop had no fancy biscuits, only basic supplies. Milk had to be fetched fresh every morning from a neighbour who owned a cow. Internet signals would vanish just when I needed them most. And sometimes, the water taps would run dry, and we had to carry buckets from a nearby spring.

But then the mountains began to work their slow magic.

The children discovered joy in running outside, chasing butterflies instead of cartoons, and climbing small hills instead of playground slides. They would come home with muddy shoes, wildflowers in their hands, and stories of the little friends they had made in the village.

My wife, who had been the strongest yet most hesitant partner in this adventure, started finding rhythm in village life — chatting with neighbours, learning recipes cooked on wood stoves, even laughing at the odd inconveniences. She once told me, with a smile I'll never forget, "It feels like we've stepped back in time… but maybe that's exactly what we needed."

And I felt something stir inside me too. A forgotten part of myself — one that was not tied to job titles, screens, or traffic jams — began to breathe again.

🌨️ Nature's Reminder: Respect the Land

One of the hardest lessons came during our first monsoon. A small stream near our rented home turned into a wild torrent overnight. A local villager told us, *"Never build or buy too close to a river. The mountain takes back what belongs to it."*
It was a reality check: that beautiful piece of land by the riverside may look like paradise in summer, but in the rainy season, it can be dangerous.

Testing Ourselves

That year was our test.

Could we live without city comforts?
Could the children adapt?
Could we survive on less income, but more meaning?

We had no answers at the start. But each day brought lessons. Some were hard, some were joyful, all were necessary.

We learned how to store water, how to cook when the power was gone, how to walk kilometres because the road was blocked, how to wake with the sun because life in the hills runs on daylight.

The children, in their own innocent way, taught us the most. They were quick to adapt. Where we saw inconvenience, they saw adventure. A sudden power cut meant candlelit games. A missing internet connection meant more time outside. A muddy path was not an obstacle but an invitation to splash and play.

And we also learned something deeper:

That life slows down here, but it never feels empty.
That silence can be frightening at first — but then it heals you.
That freedom is not the absence of responsibility, but the presence of choice.

The Year That Changed Everything

By the end of that year, something had shifted in all of us.

The children didn't want to return to the city. They had tasted the freedom of wide-open fields and the thrill of friendships without screens. My wife, who once worried about the practicality of it all, admitted she felt lighter, calmer, happier here. And I... I knew I could never go back to the old life unchanged.

The rented house had become more than a trial. It had become the doorway. We still didn't own land. We hadn't built a home yet. But in our hearts, the decision was made:

This was not just an escape. This was our future.

What Helped Us Survive the Shift

Keeping our expectations real, not romantic
Listening to locals more than Google
Accepting imperfection as normal
Preparing for winters early
Being open to failure, but also to small daily joys

That one rented home became the bridge between two worlds — the city we left behind, and the mountain life we were slowly learning to love.

It wasn't perfect. But it was enough to show us:

"Yes, we can live here"
"Yes, the children can grow here"
"Yes, this life is hard — but it feels real"

This first year was our test. And somehow, the mountains said: *"You passed."*

The Slow Search

By the end of our first year, we had realised something important: choosing a place in the mountains is not about finding the "perfect" spot. It's about finding a place where your heart feels at peace *and* your daily life feels possible.

Slowly, we began to see which region spoke to us the most.

That set the stage for the next step of our journey: not just renting, but eventually finding land to call our own.

Chapter 4: A Dream Washed Away

The Leap from Renting to Owning a Piece of the Himalayas

The rented house gave us a glimpse of mountain life — its joys and its struggles. But we knew it wasn't truly ours. It was like wearing someone else's shoes: they protected your feet, but never quite fit.

We wanted roots. A place we could call our own. A space shaped not by the choices of a landlord, but by our dreams.

That desire pushed us into the next chapter of our journey: buying land. When you decide to leave the city for the mountains, the first big question is not *what* to do — but *where* to go.

The Himalayas stretch across thousands of kilometres, each region with its own personality, challenges, and beauty. Choosing the right place is half the journey.

The mountains of India are vast and varied. From the pine-scented slopes of Himachal to the raw, ancient valleys of Kashmir, and the high meadows of Uttarakhand — each region has its own rhythm, its own challenges, and its own kind of welcome.

Our one-year rental stay became our classroom. It gave us time to explore nearby valleys, meet locals, and understand the reality of mountain life before committing to a permanent home.

The Search for a Place Called Home

In the mountains, buying land is nothing like the city. There are no glossy brochures, no online listings with wide-angle photos. Here, it's word-of-mouth, village connections, long walks up and down slopes, and endless cups of chai with people you've just met.

We searched for months. Some lands were too steep, others too far from water, and some came with disputes older than the trees that grew on them.

Every time we thought we'd found "the one," something didn't add up.

The children grew restless with our constant visits to strangers' fields. They would tug at my hand and whisper, "Papa, when will we have our own garden to play in?" My wife, ever practical, worried aloud, "Are we really sure? What if we invest and then regret it?"

But my heart kept whispering back: *If we want to grow here, we need soil of our own.*

The Himalayas receive heavy monsoons, and some regions are prone to cloudbursts and flash floods. Valleys near rivers and streams may look inviting, but they often carry hidden risks. When you're shortlisting an area, always ask locals about past flood events and seasonal water levels — these stories matter more than any brochure or government map.

When actually searching for land, avoid low-lying plots near rivers, streams, or seasonal drain channels (*naalas*). Even a small mountain stream can turn violent during monsoon, sweeping away boundary walls, crops, or even houses. Always check the water flow during rains, and if possible, visit the land in monsoon before finalising.

⚡ The Fraud

During our stay in the village, we met a man involved in property dealing and construction. He seemed well-connected and familiar with the area, and eventually showed us a plot of land that immediately caught our attention. It was peaceful, picturesque, and seemed like the perfect place to build a future. After discussing it with my parents—who also liked the idea—we asked to see the legal documents.

The seller, acting as a middleman, presented us with an agreement. As it turned out, he had purchased the land from the original owner at a lower price but hadn't yet transferred the property into his name. Despite some reservations, we decided to move forward and handed over ₹30,000 as a token amount for the plot, which was valued around ₹10 lakh. We signed a basic agreement on stamp paper in the presence of the *Ameen*—a local official responsible for verifying land measurements and maps.

Feeling optimistic, we returned home with the intention of finalising the sale within a month. This decision came after spending four meaningful months in the village, and since the seller was known to the locals, we placed a degree of trust in him.

However, life took an unexpected turn. Our children struggled to adjust to village life and deeply missed their grandparents. Around the same time, a massive flood struck the area—the gentle stream near our rented home turned into a raging river. These events forced us to return to the city.

From there, we tried repeatedly to contact the seller, requesting the official land documents—*khatauni*—and a copy of our agreement. His tone changed. He began ignoring our calls, becoming increasingly evasive and eventually, outright rude. The dream we had nurtured so carefully was slipping away.

After much deliberation and emotional exhaustion, we made a painful decision: to let go of the land and not pursue the deal any further. We realised that if we returned to demand our token money back, there was a strong chance the seller would deny it—and we'd end up spending even more time, energy, and money chasing it.

With heavy hearts, we walked away from the deal, disillusioned and disheartened. The experience taught us a hard lesson, and we vowed never again to buy land in the hills. It wasn't just the money we lost—it was a piece of our peace, and a dream that ended before it even began.

Chapter 5: Rising from the Ashes

Even broken dreams leave behind the seeds of new beginnings.

🌱 Hope & faith

Though the pain of the land deal lingered, our love for the mountains never faded. We had walked away bruised, but not broken. In quiet conversations over tea, my parents reminded us that setbacks were a part of every meaningful journey—that the mountains would wait for us, patiently, until we were ready again. Their faith rekindled something within us. Slowly, hope began to rise once more—not from dreams of ownership, but from the desire to live closer to nature, on our own terms.

With renewed determination, we returned to the mountains and began our search for land again. The fraud had shaken us, but it couldn't steal the vision we held in our hearts.

⛰ The Land That Chose Us

A few months later, while returning from a family trip to Badrinath, we passed through a small village in the Kumaon region of Uttarakhand.

The monsoon was just ending, and the valleys were bursting with lush, vibrant greenery. In that moment, the old fire within me—the deep longing to live in the hills—rekindled with a quiet but powerful glow. We stopped at a tea shop and asked the owner if he knew of any land for sale nearby. He pointed us toward a nearby land.

In the hills, it's not just about the view. We learned to ask:

"Does water reach here easily?"
"How far is the nearest road in monsoon?"
"Is the slope safe from landslides?"
"Is there a stream or nullah nearby that floods during heavy rains?"

One villager gave us priceless advice: *"Don't get fooled by sunshine days. Come see the land during the rains."* That one sentence saved us from buying in the wrong spot.

And that day, we found it. The moment we saw it, something stirred inside us. There's a saying that you don't choose the land—the land chooses you. And in that instant, we felt that call.

It wasn't perfect, the land was uneven, wild, with tall grasses waving in the wind and stones scattered like obstacles in our path.

But something about it felt alive. The sound of a nearby stream, the view of snow peaks in the distance, the smell of pine in the air — it tugged at me.

I stood there in silence, my children running freely around me, their laughter echoing in the open space, and I knew: *This was it.*

🤝 The Deal

Buying land in the hills is rarely straightforward. There were endless papers, signatures, stamps, and a dozen trips to the tehsil office. Each visit meant carrying a bag of hope, patience, and snacks for the kids, because government offices in mountain towns move slower than glaciers.

We met the landowner and had the property documents thoroughly verified by the local *Patwari*. Once we were confident everything was in order, we gave a small token amount of ₹5,000 as a gesture of commitment. This time, we were clear and firm: the full payment would only be made through a cheque in court —no cash transactions whatsoever.

The middleman involved in the deal tried to push for a larger cash advance, but we declined. Instead, we requested that he complete the fencing around the land first, which we agreed to pay for separately. Once the fencing was done and no other party came forward to claim any rights to the property, our confidence grew.

The paperwork was clean, all financial transactions were to be routed through the bank, and the deal was being made directly with the landowner—a respected and well-known figure in the village.

We had calculated every risk carefully, and this time, we moved ahead with caution and clarity.

Finally, the day arrived

we went to the court to complete the paperwork and officially register the land in our name. Around seven to eight people from the seller's family came along, each one required to sign the documents as part of the legal process. Everything went smoothly.

We received the official papers, handed over the cheque, and just like that, the dream we had once let go of had found solid ground.

Finally! we held the papers in our hands & this wild patch of Himalayan earth was now ours.

To mark the moment, we all gathered at a nearby local shop for a small tea party with hot samosas—a simple celebration that felt deeply meaningful. They say it's tradition in the hills, and in that moment, we felt like we had truly become a part of it.

Chapter 6: Building from Nothing

The real adventure begins..

Owning the land was one thing. Building a home on it was another mountain altogether and came the real adventure.

💪 The Real Challenge

The desire to build our home in the hills grew stronger with each passing day— but I must admit, it turned out to be one of the greatest challenges of my life.

Building a house in the mountains is not just about money; in fact, the financial aspect is only one piece of a far more complex puzzle.

What truly matters is finding a trustworthy builder, nurturing good relationships with neighbours and locals, understanding the weather patterns, and respecting the unique nature of the land itself.

I learned the hard way that if you don't belong to the hills—if you're an outsider—building a home there can cost you more than money. It can test your peace of mind, shake your sense of stability, and leave behind scars on your soul that may never fully heal.

In the mountains, building is twice as challenging as in the city:

Materials are harder to transport.
Skilled masons are few — and often booked months ahead. Weather delays everything.

We designed our home simple, functional, and with local wisdom:

A sloping tin roof to handle snow and rain.

Stone walls for insulation.

A veranda for sitting, drying crops, and greeting neighbours.

Every stone laid was a milestone. Every day, we watched our dream take shape — not in a brochure-perfect way, but in a raw, real, and sturdy way.

We didn't hire a big city architect. Instead, we spoke with local masons and carpenters, men whose knowledge came not from books but from years of shaping stone and wood with their hands. They told us what the land could hold, how the walls should breathe, how the roof must bend to the snow.

I designed the house myself, with careful thought and intention. It was important to build on the flattest part of the land, safely away from the mountain slope and at a comfortable distance from the road. I chose to keep the structure simple and modest—not just to manage costs, but because my priority was to move in as soon as possible. This wasn't about luxury or grandeur; it was about creating a safe, peaceful space in the hills that felt like home from the very beginning.

While our home was being built, we rented a small one-bedroom place nearby that included a kitchen. Staying close allowed us to oversee the construction closely and be part of every step as our dream home slowly took shape.

We inquired at a local school for our children's admission. Although the school had very basic infrastructure, our options were limited in the area.

We decided that, alongside their regular schooling, we would dedicate extra time ourselves to support and guide their education at home. With that plan in place, the admission process was completed.

The children would watch the workers pile stones into walls and ask, "Papa, when will our house be ready?" My wife, balancing between excitement and worry, would help me bargain for cement one day and sketch room layouts with me the next.

Money was always tight. Every extra wall or window felt like a debate between dream and reality.

But slowly, stone by stone, beam by beam, our dream began to take shape.

🏡 The Day It Became Home

After a year and a half of hard work and patience, our small home was finally ready to welcome us. It had a cozy bedroom, a combined living room and kitchen, a washroom, and a modest attic to accommodate a few more guests.

Though simple, it was everything we had hoped for—a true sanctuary in the hills where new memories could begin.

I still remember the first night we slept in our own house. There was no paint yet, the wiring was half-done, and the roof still leaked in one corner. But it was ours.

Unlike the rented house, this one carried our sweat, our risk, and our faith. The walls were not just stone and cement — they were a declaration: *We belong here.*

we celebrated with a simple, light party. Without furniture in place, we slept on floor mattresses, embracing the rawness of the moment.

Over the next few days, we bought a few chairs for both indoors and outdoors, slowly making the space our own. It was harvesting season for peaches and plums, and we delighted in tasting the first fruits from our land—peaches larger than apples and plums so ripe they melted on the tongue.

Our farm had over a hundred fruit trees when we bought it, along with several majestic oak trees surrounding the property. The weather was perfect—fresh mountain air, no pollution, no scorching summer heat, and cool, crisp nights. For our family, this was more than a dream come true; it was a milestone to celebrate and cherish forever.

Chapter 7: Life in Harmony: Embraced by Nature

Discovering the true meaning of home and togetherness

Our daily routine soon settled into a beautiful rhythm—waking up to the songs of birds, stepping out for morning walks, exchanging warm hellos with the locals along the way. After breakfast, we would drop the kids at school and then tend to the farm.

Most of our days were filled with planting saplings, watering crops, sowing seeds, clearing bushes, and cooking on the traditional *chulha*, an Indian wood-fire stove. Birds of all kinds filled the skies and trees—both local residents and migratory visitors.

The morning mist often wrapped the valley like a playful game of hide and seek, enchanting us with its quiet magic.

Villagers frequently stopped by to chat and hear about our experiences. My wife made daily trips into the village for fresh cow's milk, while the kids gradually settled in, playing with local children and inviting them over to our farm.

The seasonal fruits we tasted were unlike anything we had ever experienced. Time passed swiftly, and we found ourselves completely immersed in the gentle embrace of nature.

The First Winter

By the time the house was livable, winter had arrived. The walls still smelled of fresh lime plaster, the floors felt cold under our feet, and the roof creaked under the weight of snow. But it was *ours*.

That first winter, we huddled together under blankets, sipping tea while the wind howled outside. The children giggled at the sound of snowflakes tapping the windows. My wife looked at me and said softly, "We've really done it, haven't we?"

And in that moment, I realized:

We weren't just building a house. We were building a life.

Roots in the Mountains

With a home of our own, everything changed. Neighbours came with baskets of fruit to welcome us. Village children knocked at our door to invite ours to play. Slowly, we were no longer "the outsiders renting a place." We were becoming part of the community.

The land that once felt wild and uncertain began to carry our fingerprints — in the small vegetable patch we planted, in the flowers my wife grew by the entrance, in the little corner where the children made a swing from a tree branch.

This was no longer a dream. It was reality.

Owning land and building a home in the mountains is not about possession — it's about commitment. It ties you to the land, the people, and the rhythm of nature. It is harder than renting, but infinitely more rewarding.

For us, the day our home stood complete was the day the mountains stopped being a dream and became our forever.

Chapter 8: The Himalayan Tsunami

The Day Nature Turned Fierce - *Everything washed away*

🌧 Catastrophe Strikes

For those seeking solace in these majestic hills, it's not just about building a home; it's about respecting a fragile ecosystem that fights back when pushed too far.

Settling here means embracing both the breathtaking beauty and the raw, sometimes unforgiving power of nature—reminding us that our future in the mountains depends on how gently we tread today.

The weather took a sudden and devastating turn. In October—when such heavy rains were unexpected—the skies opened up and relentless rain poured down for three days straight.

The local streams, *gadheras*, and rivers swelled beyond their banks, flooding everything in their path. One night, a catastrophic cloudburst struck, washing away entire valleys—homes, people, animals, and farmlands alike.

I witnessed the aftermath myself on a trip to the market the next morning. Returning home, I was met with a terrifying sight: the access path to our farmhouse was slipping away before my eyes.

A landslide was unfolding on our land, and there was nothing I could do to stop it.

The once-familiar road to our home had turned into rubble, completely washed away. My wife stood outside, tears streaming down her face, unable to join me as I climbed half a kilometre along a precarious back path to reach the house.

Our water tank had been swept away, and within hours, we were left without water, electricity, road access, or medical assistance. Everyone around us was struggling with their own losses—there was no one to turn to for help.

News of the disaster spread worldwide, with roads washed away across the district and countless families mourning loved ones lost in this unimaginable catastrophe.

The Himalayas, once a timeless sanctuary of peace and balance, are now whispering a warning—one that no newcomer can afford to ignore.

The fierce storms, sudden landslides, and unpredictable weather are the scars of a changing climate, shaking the very ground beneath our dreams.

💧 The Thirst That Tested Us

After the catastrophe, the main government water supply line was completely wiped out by the flash floods. For the entire next year, we lived without a regular source of water.

Every day became a struggle—carrying heavy cans to a distant local water source, filling them, and making the long journey back home. Water, once taken for granted, became the hardest battle we faced. Local suppliers charged as much as 2,000 rupees for a 2,000-litre tank, barely enough to last a few days.

I even created a temporary access path with just a shovel and stones, carving a fragile route from the road to our sanctuary—our hope still alive amidst the struggle.

Chapter 9: Challenges vs. Rewards

The Balance Sheet of Mountain Life

If life in the hills could be written as an account book, it would not show only profit or only loss. It is always a balance sheet — where struggles and blessings sit on either side. Some days the challenges weigh heavier, other days the rewards sparkle brighter. But together, they make mountain life complete.

The Challenges

The cold in winter is not the "turn up the heater" kind of cold. It seeps into your bones. Water freezes in the pipes, doors swell with moisture, and every small task — from bathing to washing clothes — becomes an act of endurance.

A sudden landslide can block the only road to the village. A storm can bring down power lines for days. A stream that looked harmless in summer can turn into a raging torrent during the monsoon. Living here means accepting that nature is not always your friend.

If you need a doctor at midnight, there is no 24-hour hospital around the corner. If your child falls sick, you sometimes pray more than you depend on medicine. Grocery shopping is not about convenience stores — it's about planning in advance, because the nearest market might be two hours away.

Despite the beauty, isolation is real. Friends from the city call less often. Relatives visit rarely. Festivals are quieter. And sometimes, in that silence, you question: *Did I choose too much solitude?*

The Rewards

In the city, nights are painted with neon lights. Here, the sky reveals itself in all its glory. Millions of stars, the Milky Way stretching above, the silence only broken by the call of an owl. That sight alone makes every hardship worth it.

In the city, gadgets kept us apart. In the mountains, shared struggles brought us closer. Collecting firewood together, waiting out storms under one roof, laughing when things went wrong — these moments stitched us as a family in ways the city never could.

Neighbours here are not just neighbours. They are family without blood ties. When your roof leaks, someone comes with tools. When their cow falls sick, you offer help. In joy and in sorrow, you stand together.

This spirit of belonging is priceless.

Perhaps the greatest reward is invisible. It is the quiet confidence that grows in you when you face challenges

and still wake up each morning with gratitude. It is the peace of knowing you are where you are meant to be.

⚖️ The Balance

Whenever people ask me, *"Was it worth it? Leaving the city, the comforts, the career?"* I smile. Because no balance sheet can fully capture what the mountains give back.

Yes, there are struggles — sometimes painful, sometimes frightening. But every time I sit on my porch and see the sun rise over the ridges, every time my children laugh freely in the open air, I know the rewards far outweigh the challenges.

In the end, the mountains test you, shape you, and then reward you in ways that money or comfort never can.

Chapter 10: Building the Connection

The Heartbeat of Mountain Life

Mountains are not just about peaks and valleys. They are about people. And without winning their trust, no one truly survives here.

🌱 The First Steps

When we built our home in the village, I felt like an outsider. The locals looked at us with curiosity — city people trying to play mountain life. At first, conversations were brief, polite, distant. I realised quickly: respect is not given here, it is earned.

It started with small gestures — greeting elders with folded hands, buying vegetables from the village women instead of bringing everything from the town, sitting on the ground in their kitchens and drinking tea without hurry.
Each small act whispered, *"I am here not above you, but among you."*

The Bonds That Matter

One day, when our house construction was at its peak, unexpected rain poured down, threatening to wash away the newly dug foundation. Before I could panic, half a dozen villagers appeared — some with shovels, some with tarpaulin sheets. They worked as if it were their own home.

That night I realised: in the mountains, survival is always collective.

Later, when my children started playing with local kids, walls broke even faster. Laughter is the strongest bridge — and children build it without effort.

Through them, we found family friends, shared meals, and invitations to weddings and festivals.

🎶 Learning Their Way

The beauty of these connections was not one-sided. We learned so much:

How to grow rajma and potatoes in terraced fields.
Which wild herbs cure a cough or a stomach ache.
Why certain rituals before sowing or harvesting are sacred.

At first, I smiled politely at these traditions. Later, I realised they were not superstitions — they were centuries of wisdom wrapped in culture.

Respect, Always

It wasn't always smooth. Misunderstandings happened — sometimes about land boundaries, sometimes about city habits that clashed with local ways.

But the lesson was clear: humility always wins. When you admit your mistakes, when you listen more than you speak, trust deepens.

Today, when I walk through the village, I am not "the outsider who built a house." I am "bhaiya" or "dost." That shift in identity is not just sweet — it is survival itself.

The Heartbeat

Looking back, I realise: the heart of mountain life does not beat in the forests or rivers, but in the homes of its people. Without them, the mountains can be lonely, even hostile. With them, every hardship becomes lighter, every festival brighter, every day warmer.

Building connections with locals was not an option. It was the key that unlocked the true mountain life we had been seeking all along.

Chapter 11: When the Mountains Gave Back

Finding Our Way to Make a Living

When we packed our bags and left the city, there was one question that kept following us like a shadow:

"But how will you earn in the mountains?"

Friends asked it. Relatives repeated it. Even in my own heart, it echoed quietly. After all, life in the city may have been suffocating—but it was safe.

The salary came on the 1st, bills were paid, and everything ran on schedule. In the hills, we were stepping into the unknown.

The Pause Before the Leap

During our first year in the rented house, we didn't rush into anything. It would have been easy to jump into some business idea, but instead we chose to watch, listen, and understand.

We spent our days walking through villages, sitting with locals, hearing about their work. Some families depended on orchards, others on seasonal tourism. Many still grew their own food.

Almost everyone had more than one way of earning—because the mountains demand flexibility.

That year became our education.

The Dream of Our Own Land

When we finally bought land and built our home, the question of livelihood returned, louder this time. This was not just a year's experiment anymore. This was us putting down roots.

I remember standing on the half-built verandah of our new home, looking at the valley, and asking myself—*what can we do here, honestly and sustainably?*

The answer came slowly, in layers.

The Hachi

The children longed for a true companion, so we brought home a Siberian Husky as a gift for them. We named him Hachi, after the famous dog Hachiko, though he was an Akita. Hachi quickly became a beloved member of our family, joining us in every adventure.

He accompanied the kids on nature trails and always kept us alert whenever wildlife was nearby.

Opening Our Doors: The Homestay

Our first step was to open a small homestay.

As our connection with the mountains deepened, we decided to expand our little home. We added two more rooms, thoughtfully designed, so that we could welcome guests and share the beauty of our life in the hills.

The idea of turning our home into a homestay wasn't just about hosting—it was about offering others a chance to experience the peace, simplicity, and raw charm that had transformed us.

We didn't plan it as a business at first. It was just that friends who visited never wanted to leave. They loved the simplicity of village life, the vegetables we picked straight from the garden, the warmth of the kitchen fire in the evenings.

So we thought—why not open our doors to others too?

The rooms were basic, the food homely, but what guests valued most was the authenticity. They weren't just tourists; they became part of our story for a few days. Some still call us years later, saying the silence of our village changed something inside them.

Running a homestay wasn't without challenges—fixing water pipes, managing electricity cuts, balancing our own privacy. But it gave us both an income and a way to share what we loved about this life.

The Unexpected Path: YouTube

Alongside the homestay, another door opened—one I hadn't imagined before moving.

I began sharing our journey on my YouTube channel, *Punjabi Trekker*. At first, it was just simple videos: the morning light on snow peaks, the sound of the river, the struggles of carrying supplies up steep paths.

To my surprise, people connected. Viewers from cities wrote, saying they lived this life through our videos. Some asked practical questions about shifting to the hills. Others just wanted to hear the wind in the pines.

Slowly, that channel became more than just a diary. It brought in a little income, yes—but more importantly, it gave our story wings. It made me realize that even in the remoteness of the mountains, you can still reach the world.

Growing from the Soil

And then, there was the land itself.

The first time I dug the soil to plant potatoes an, I felt a kind of freedom that no city job had ever given me. The harvest was small, sometimes uneven, but each meal cooked from our own garden carried a pride money couldn't buy.

We sold a little extra produce here and there, but more than income, farming gave us independence. It taught us that in the mountains, wealth is not measured in bank accounts alone—it is also in jars of rajma, in baskets of apples, in the laughter of neighbours helping each other in the fields.

Lessons the Hills Taught Us About Money

The mountains don't allow greed. They teach you to earn *enough*, not endlessly. Income here is rarely steady. Some months are abundant; some are lean. You learn to live with both.

Work is woven with life—you don't "go to office," your livelihood grows around your home, your land, your community.

Looking back, I see now that the question "How will you earn?" was never just about money. It was about survival, dignity, and purpose.

In the city, earning had been about climbing ladders. Here, it became about planting roots. And in that shift—from chasing more to cherishing enough—we found not just a livelihood, but a life.

Chapter 12: Feeding Life from the Soil

How We Learned to Grow Our Own Food in the Hills

When we first moved to the mountains, food was one of our biggest questions.
Would we be able to grow our own?

Could we reduce our dependence on markets that were often far away and unreliable?

It wasn't about becoming completely self-sufficient — but about tasting the joy of eating something that came from our own soil, touched by our own hands.

I began learning farming skills I had never imagined I would need. Who would have thought that a software architect would one day become a farmer? But strangely, it felt natural. I found peace in the slow rhythm of farm life—working the soil felt like being cradled in the lap of Mother Nature herself. In time, I was able to plough fields with just a shovel and transform them into thriving vegetable gardens.

My wife was equally committed and I learned many practical skills from her. Looking back, I know this move to the mountains would never have been possible without her unwavering support and the quiet strength of our family standing behind us.

🌱 The First Patch of Soil

I still remember the day we cleared a small patch near our new home. The soil was rocky, with pebbles hidden beneath the surface. My children were excited, treating it like playtime, digging with sticks, while my wife and I tried to loosen the stubborn earth.

We started small — just a few spinach plants, some potatoes, and coriander. The first attempt wasn't impressive. Some seeds didn't sprout, a few leaves were eaten by insects, and the potatoes were laughably tiny. But the taste of that first spinach leaf, grown right outside our door, was unlike anything I had eaten before. It wasn't just food — it was a connection.

🍅 Learning from Locals

Soon, we realised we needed help. The villagers had been farming for generations, and every conversation with them was like opening a book of wisdom.

"Don't plant tomatoes before mid-April; the frost will take them."
"Mix cow dung with dry leaves for stronger soil."
"Always build channels to guide rainwater — or it will wash everything away."

Slowly, we began to understand the rhythm of the land

🥔 What Worked for Us

We learned that mountain soil is best for hardy crops — potatoes, beans, spinach, peas, radish, and seasonal vegetables. My children loved seeing the pea pods grow, often plucking them raw and eating them on the spot. We also planted fruit trees — apples, plums, apricots, peaches — knowing they would take years to bear fruit, but believing in the long patience of mountain life.

🌧️ Failures and Small Victories

There were many failures. Heavy rains once washed away an entire patch of seedlings. Monkeys raided our maize field. Sometimes, a whole season felt wasted. But then there were moments — like when we harvested a sack of potatoes that actually lasted us through winter, or when my wife made chutney with fresh coriander from our garden — that reminded us why we started.

🌿 The Joy Beyond Food

Growing food was never just about filling our plates. It became therapy.

After a long day of work, stepping into the garden, watering plants, feeling the soil in our hands — it grounded us. It gave our children lessons no school could teach. They learned patience, care, and the reward of watching something grow slowly, silently, yet surely.

And every time we sit down to eat a meal that has even a little from our land — a potato, a tomato, a handful of greens — it feels like a prayer of gratitude to the mountains for allowing us to be here.

Chapter 13 - Living on the Edge: Between the Thirst, Frost & Forrest

Dealing with the Tough Stuff

When people see the mountains on YouTube or in tourist brochures, they see peace: waterfalls, snowy peaks, and pine forests swaying in the wind. But behind that postcard beauty lies the other side of reality — the challenges that test your patience, your body, and sometimes even your spirit.

For us, three things stood out above all: water, winters, and wildlife.

💧 Water – A Daily Struggle

In the city, water came from a tap. Here, it came from the mountain. Sometimes a trickle, sometimes not at all.

The first summer after moving in, our spring dried up. We carried buckets from a neighbour's source half a kilometre away. My children, who once turned on taps without thinking, learned to measure every drop. My wife began storing water in barrels, teaching us the meaning of conservation.

And in winter? The pipes froze. On some mornings, I remember breaking ice just to fill a pot for tea.

It was frustrating at first, but slowly, we adapted. We learned to store enough before nightfall, to insulate pipes with cloth, and to always keep a bucket ready indoors.

Lesson: In the mountains, water isn't free. It is precious, sacred, and demands respect.

❄️ Winters – The Season of Endurance

If water was our summer challenge, winter was a test of everything else.

The first snowfall felt magical — until the power went out for three days. The house turned colder than the outside, and we burned wood late into the night. Supplies ran low. Roads were blocked.

The children missed school for weeks. I will never forget carrying sacks of flour on my back after a neighbour arranged some from town.

But something else happened too. We began sitting closer, talking longer, laughing more around the fire. Winters forced us to pause, to survive together as a family. They built resilience in the children and patience in us as parents.

Lesson: Winters are not just cold; they are teachers. They teach humility, preparation, and gratitude.

🐾 Wildlife – Sharing the Hills

Then came the unexpected guests — the real natives of the mountains.

Living amidst raw, untamed nature brought us face to face with the true wilderness. Leopards, snakes, wild hogs, and even bears roamed the area, reminding us daily that we were guests in their territory.

I had to reinforce the fencing around our farm to keep it secure, and one unspoken rule quickly became clear—never step out alone after 7 PM.

At night, the silence was often broken by rustling bushes or the distant, haunting cry of a barking deer under attack by a leopard.

Our husky, full of spirit and strength, had to be kept indoors after 5 PM, the very hour when predators often prowled for goats—or dogs.

At night, the dogs barked at shadows. Once, a leopard took a goat from a neighbour's shed. In summer, bears wandered close, searching for food. Snakes slithered in the fields, and monkeys often raided our vegetables before we could harvest them.

Fear was natural. But over time, we learned respect.

We built stronger fencing. We avoided leaving food outside. We taught our children not to run if they saw an animal but to stay calm and come inside.

And yet, despite the risks, there is awe in seeing a wild animal in its home. A reminder that we are the outsiders here.
The mountains are not ours to tame — they are ours to live with, carefully.

Lesson: Living in the hills means sharing space with those who were here long before us. This life in the mountains taught us more than decades in the city ever could.

It was wild, real, and humbling. Our children began to absorb the skills and resilience required to live a true *Pahadi* life. The mountains make you tough—or they send you back.

The mountains are not only beautiful — they are demanding. They strip away comfort and force you to face what really matters.

They are not a place for the weak of will or heart. Here, the mountains are not just geography—they are gods. And if you cannot respect nature, then nature will not make space for you.

Water shortages, frozen winters, and wildlife encounters are not "problems" anymore. They are part of our life, stitched into our story.

And every time I face them, I remember why we came here: not for an easy life, but for a true one.

Chapter 14: Raising a Family here

Education, Healthcare, Community, Kids' Freedom

When we first dreamt of moving to the mountains, our biggest hesitation wasn't money or weather. It was our children.

Would they find good schools? Would they feel isolated? Would they resent us later for taking them away from the city's comforts?

These questions stayed in our hearts long before we packed our bags.

🎒 The School Search

After we bought land and started building our home, we began looking seriously at schools.

The nearest government school was just a walk away, but its facilities were limited. Private schools in the region were better, though often far and with basic infrastructure compared to city standards.

I still remember visiting one school where the teacher, in between classes, was also helping repair a broken chair. Something about that image stayed with me — the honesty of it, the "do-it-yourself" spirit.

We eventually chose a small private school that balanced academics with care.

The children didn't get the latest gadgets or plush classrooms, but they gained something else: attention, values, and friendships rooted in simplicity.

I still recall the first day of school. My son clutched my hand tightly, looking at the small playground and whispering, "Papa, is this really my school?" It was so different from the big, bright city buildings he knew.

But within a week, he came running home with stories of chasing goats on the way back and how the teacher told him tales of the Himalayas. Slowly, curiosity replaced hesitation.

My daughter too struggled at first with the slower pace and fewer facilities.

But she found joy in things the city never gave her: picking wildflowers for her teacher, walking with friends through pine forests, and studying under open skies during power cuts.

A Family's Test

As we began settling into our new village life, the thought of our children's education was always in the background. We didn't want them to fall behind, so we came up with an idea—why not invite someone from the city, a good teacher with a dream of living close to nature in the mountains? We could help him and his family relocate, find a rental home, and provide all the support they needed.

This way, not only our children but many others in the village could benefit from quality education.

With this thought in mind, I spoke to my cousin, who was a teacher and ran a small institute in the city. He liked the idea, and since he was self-employed, the move was not too difficult for him professionally.

But moving to the mountains was an entirely different challenge. He worried about whether his family would be able to adjust to the new lifestyle. Would there be enough income to cover groceries and rent? Could they truly adapt to this life?

In the end, his love for nature and the promise of a new beginning gave him the courage to try.

We found him a comfortable rental home near the school, and soon he began tutoring the village children. They were overjoyed to learn from an experienced teacher from the city.

At first, life seemed like a dream for his family—fresh mountain air, pure spring water, organic vegetables, and breathtaking views. But as time passed, challenges began to surface.

The rains would sometimes continue for a week, flash floods struck nearby, and their children started missing relatives and friends back in the city.

His wife too longed for the company of family. After a few months, the weight of these struggles grew heavy, and they decided to return to their city home.

This is why I say—mountain life is not for everyone. It is only for those who dare to live like a mountain itself: strong, patient, and unshaken.

🏥 Health Concerns

Healthcare was another big worry. In the hills, the nearest hospital is often an at least two hours away. In emergencies, that distance feels endless.

We prepared ourselves:

A good first-aid kit at home.
Learning basic remedies from local elders.
Building relationships with doctors in the nearest town.

Yes, it's a compromise compared to city hospitals, but it also taught us to be more mindful of our health and lifestyle. The clean air, the walks, the food we grew — they became our preventive medicine.

🏡 A Childhood of Freedom

What the children lost in malls and multiplexes, they gained in trees, rivers, and fields. I would watch them climb apple trees, chase butterflies, or come home with muddy shoes and glowing smiles.

They learned patience when seedlings sprouted, courage when thunderstorms roared, and kindness from the local community who treated them as their own.

One memory I treasure deeply is of the monsoon season. While I worried about landslides, the kids turned the rain into play. They built little paper boats and raced them down the overflowing gullies.

Their laughter rang louder than the thunder, and in that moment I realised — they were not just adjusting, they were thriving.

Sometimes they did miss the city — the cousins, the ice-cream parlours, the endless entertainment. But slowly, they began to discover a different richness. And as parents, we found joy in watching them grow closer to nature, and to themselves.

👩‍👩‍👦 The Role of Family

Through all of this, my wife's support was the backbone. She managed the household when I was learning to fix roofs or arrange water, and she stood steady during my moments of doubt.

It wasn't always easy for her either — she too had left friends, routines, and conveniences behind. But she adapted with grace. Together, we became each other's anchor.

I remember once, during a particularly cold winter, when the water pipes froze. I felt frustrated, questioning if we had made the right choice.

My wife quietly lit the stove, warmed water for everyone, and said, "We came here for peace, not for perfection." That single sentence grounded me — reminding me that family, not circumstances, defines comfort.

🌿 Looking Back

Raising a family in the mountains isn't just about logistics — it's about building resilience, creativity, and community. There are days of frustration when the internet is down or when the road is blocked by landslides.

But there are also evenings when the children's laughter echoes through the valley, and we sit together by a wood stove, knowing we've chosen a life of depth over ease.

And that, for us, has been worth everything.

From Hesitation to Belonging

The real miracle of this journey has been watching the children's hearts change over the years. At first, they longed for their city friends, cartoons on fast internet, and big birthday parties.

There were moments of tears, especially during festivals when cousins celebrated together in Delhi while we lit diyas quietly in the hills.

But slowly, the mountains began to work their magic. The friends they made here weren't just classmates — they were playmates who shared fields, festivals, and long walks home. The festivals may have been small, but they were heartfelt — the whole village coming together with songs, dances, and food.

One day, when my son was about ten, a visiting relative asked him, "Don't you miss the city?" He looked up, thought for a while, and replied, "In the city, I had playgrounds. Here, the mountains are my playground." That was the day I knew he had accepted this life as his own.

My daughter, too, began to shine in ways I hadn't imagined. She once told me, while carrying a basket of wildflowers home, "Papa, here even the silence speaks." It was such a simple sentence, but it captured everything — the way the hills had seeped into her spirit.

Now, when we occasionally visit the city, the children enjoy the malls and lights for a few days. But after a while, they always say, "Let's go back home." And by *home*, they don't mean the city anymore. They mean the little house we built in the mountains, surrounded by pine trees and stars.

🩶 Closing Thought

For me, that is the greatest reward of all. Not just that we found peace, but that our children learned to see beauty in simplicity, strength in challenges, and joy in nature.

The mountains didn't just give us a home. They gave my children roots — and wings.

Chapter 15: The Mental Shift

From City Mindset to Mountain Mindset

When I dreamed of leaving the city, I thought the hardest part would be the physical things: buying land, building a home, surviving winters. I was wrong. The real challenge was not outside — it was inside.

Moving to the mountains is not just a change of address. It is a change of mind, of habits, of expectations. And for me, this mental shift was the biggest mountain to climb.

Letting Go of the City Pace

In the city, everything is about speed. Fast internet, fast food, fast cars, fast answers. If something takes time, we get irritated. If the electricity goes for half an hour, it feels like a crisis.

But in the village, nothing moves at that pace. If the mason doesn't show up today, you wait.

If the road is blocked due to landslide, you wait. If the internet goes for a week, you learn to live without it.

At first, I used to get restless. My city self wanted efficiency, deadlines, quick solutions. But slowly, the mountains taught me patience.

They whispered: *"Time is not running away. Slow down. Breathe."*

💸 Redefining Success

In the city, success was measured in square feet, salary slips, promotions, and possessions.

I used to think of my career ladder, of cars, of foreign holidays. That was the definition of "making it."

But here, success began to mean something else.

👉 A clear sunrise after a storm.
👉 A good harvest of vegetables from our patch of land
👉 My children walking safely back from school.
👉 Sharing tea with a neighbour who treated me like family.

One day, sitting on the porch of my unfinished home, drinking tea in a steel cup, I realised: I was happier here with less than I had ever been with more.

That was the day my definition of success changed forever.

🧘 Facing Yourself in Silence

The mountains also strip away the noise. In the city, even silence is loud — the hum of traffic, the buzz of electricity, the constant background chatter. Here, real silence exists.

At first, that silence can be uncomfortable. You face your own thoughts, your own fears, your own doubts. There's no escape into shopping malls or movie theatres. You can't drown your loneliness in distractions.

But if you sit with it long enough, the silence becomes a teacher. It teaches you to listen — to birds, to rivers, to your children's laughter, and most importantly, to yourself.

🏔 Strength in Simplicity

The biggest mental shift is learning that life does not have to be complicated to be fulfilling. The village women carrying water every morning had more strength in their smiles than many stressed professionals I knew in the city.

The farmers celebrating after a simple harvest feast had more joy than people cutting cakes in five-star hotels.

Simplicity is not poverty. Simplicity is freedom.

🩶 Closing Thought

Looking back, I often ask myself: *Did the mountains change me, or did they reveal who I always was?*

Maybe it is both. The city taught me how to run. The mountains taught me how to stop. And in stopping, I finally began to live.

Chapter 16: Is This Life for You?

An Honest Reflection Before You Take the Leap

When I first thought about leaving the city, the idea was wrapped in romance — pine forests, fresh air, birdsong at dawn.

But once you stand on the other side, you realise that the mountains test you in ways you never imagined. And before you take that leap, it's worth asking yourself: *Is this life truly for me?*

🌲 The Reality Behind the Dream

Living in the hills is not a permanent vacation. It's collecting firewood when the wind is icy. It's waking up at 5 AM because the water tank fills only at that hour. It's facing power cuts in the middle of winter nights when the children are shivering.

At the same time, it's also sipping hot tea while clouds drift through your verandah, watching your children run free in safe fields, and feeling your own heartbeat finally slow down after years of city rush.

This life is both — beauty and burden. The question is: can you embrace both with equal love?

🔎 A Simple Self-Test

Before you decide, here are a few questions to sit with honestly:

"Do you crave modern comforts more, or do you find joy in adjusting to nature's rhythm?"
"Are you ready to depend on neighbours, and be depended on, in ways city life never required?"
"Can you live with slower internet, slower roads, slower everything — without frustration?"
"Are you okay with unpredictability — from sudden weather to delayed supplies — without panicking?"

"Are you moving towards something (peace, growth, contribution) or simply away from something (stress, noise, problems)?"

The answers don't have to be perfect. But they should be honest.

🌟 Encouragement for the Brave Heart

If these questions don't scare you but instead excite you, then perhaps the mountains are calling you, too. Don't expect perfection — expect transformation.
Because this journey doesn't just change your address. It changes your mindset. It rewires what you value, what you measure success by, and how you live each day.

And here's the truth: you don't need to have all the answers before you begin. You just need the courage to start, the humility to learn, and the heart to keep going when it gets tough.

🩶 My Reflection

When I began, I had doubts. Would my children adjust? Would my wife regret the move? Would I break under the weight of unknown challenges?

But I realised something — the mountains don't demand that you be fearless. They only ask that you be willing. If you are willing to learn, to bend, to adapt, then the mountains will slowly open their arms and accept you.

Chapter 17: Where the Journey Became Life

The Journey Within

When I look back at the path that led me here, it feels less like a decision and more like destiny. From the noise of the city, the rush of deadlines, and the walls of concrete, I had once longed for a place where life could breathe — slowly, deeply, fully. The mountains answered that call.

But I realise now: the move was never just about changing geography. It was about changing myself.

🌿 The Struggles That Shaped Us

Yes, it was hard. The biting winters, the unreliable water supply, the sudden landslides, the loneliness of nights when city friends seemed worlds away. There were times I questioned everything — *Had I made a mistake?*

Yet each struggle carved us into something stronger. We learned to value less and live more.

We discovered resilience not in books, but in firewood collected before the storm, in hands calloused from work, in children laughing even when power cuts turned the nights dark.

🏡 A Family's Journey

This journey was never mine alone. My wife's patience, her steady encouragement, her ability to make a simple meal feel like a feast — that was the backbone of our survival. My children, who adjusted to new schools, made new friends, and taught me what adaptation really means, were the reason we kept going.

Family was not left behind in the city. Family was the reason this dream stood tall in the mountains.

🌄 Finding Belonging

Somewhere along the way, we stopped being "visitors." The locals became our teachers, friends, and protectors. Their wisdom filled gaps that books could never cover. Their warmth made this land feel like home.

I came here searching for peace in nature. I found it also in people.

💛 The Call of the Mountains

The title of this book — *Mountain Calling* — was not chosen lightly. Because the truth is, mountains don't call everyone. And when they do, you must listen carefully.

The call is not about escape, but about return — a return to simplicity, to community, to the self you had forgotten in the chaos of city life.

To You, Dear Reader

If you, too, feel the tug of that call but journey may not be easy. It will demand patience, courage, and sacrifice. But it will also give you something the city never can: a life lived close to the earth, to the sky, and to your own soul.

As I sit on my verandah today, watching the sun slip behind the Himalayan ridges, I know one thing with certainty — I am home. Not just in a house, not just in a village, but in a way of life that feels truer than anything I left behind.

The mountains are no longer calling.
They have spoken. And I have answered.

www.ingramcontent.com/pod-product-compliance
Ingram Content Group UK Ltd.
Pitfield, Milton Keynes, MK11 3LW, UK
UKHW021836071225
9418UKWH00030B/743

9 789334 391725